The Undoing

The Undoing

BRIAN VANDERLIP

Netherlandic Press, 1994
Windsor, Ontario

CANADIAN CATALOGUING IN PUBLICATION DATA

Vanderlip, Brian
  The undoing

Poems.
ISBN 0-919417-37-X

I. Title.

PS8593.A53863U5   1994   C811'.54   C94-932219-9
PR9199.3.V3U5   1994

Published by Netherlandic Press, P.O. Box 396, Station A,
Windsor, Ontario, Canada N9A 6L7.

The publisher wishes to acknowledge the generous financial
support of the Canada Council and the Ontario Arts Council –
Joan Magee, Publisher.

Thanks to Gerard Brender à Brandis for permission to reproduce
the wood engraving 'Tulip' on the back cover of this book.

The cover painting, *By The Breath of The Spirit* II, is by William
Kurelek. It is reproduced courtesy of The Isaacs Gallery, Toronto.
By permission of the Estate of William Kurelek.

for Donna

CONTENTS

3 Dangling Affirmations

He who is outside the door
has already a good part of his journey behind him.
— Dutch proverb

Burnham Beach Lessons

Eight or nine years old
bewitched, eager
to fulfill the darker scriptures
preached into childhood
I found the flame
and scorched everything with it
initials in fenceposts
dark carved cryptics
on hardcover school books
insects chased down
till they curled and popped
out of themselves
in a whiff of acrid smoke
searching the mystery of things
crushing and setting blazes
for Jesus:
Destruction is so religious
every fervent child of God
an armed crusader
magnifier held high
burning down the outside
and the in.

Ten-year-olds
a dozen of us lined up
at the front of the church
because the world
just might end today
and we have all sinned
Romans 3, verse 23
our fisted, hounded hearts
and the preacher
offering one last chance.
Streets paved with gold
stream liquid
through amber
stained-glass windows.
Some of us softly weep
awful doubt in ourselves
our Baptist Jesus
and the preacher walking
our line and shaking hands
as if we were grownup
and big enough to deal
with being caught
between heaven and hell
on a Sunday morning
and our walking right
into the arms of it
idiot-faced
crying along with the music.

All the good bad people have come to ask forgiveness and get right
with God again. My mother sits in the pew with her children,
dabbing her damp forehead with the balled up kleenex she hides
in her palm or under the cuff of her sleeve. We are watching my
father in his pulpit because he is angry: too many people have
sinned and not appreciated Jesus hanging on the Cross for them.
And the Devil is roaming around.

It's not that I refuse to listen to my father's sermon: it's Christ's
blood that draws my attention away. I close my eyes and see him
hanging on a telephone post, hands crushed with railway spikes,
blood dripping into snaking, little puffs of smoke as it hits the
dusty ground.

These days are the last ones: the sun is going to explode and
people won't be safe in their old bomb-shelters or down in their
basements. The sun is going to burst, like oil on the stove
catching fire and being thrown on your bare skin. Only the
Fellowship Baptists will escape when they are grabbed by God
just before it happens. One minute, a child will be playing and the
next, only his shoes will remain. God will sweep him away faster
than a blink of an eye. The outsiders and heathens will be left
staring at the Baptists' empty shoes until the hot oil burns
everyone to a crisp.

When we get home mother puts the roasted chicken on the table for our Sunday meal. Hell is probably a lot like the stove when you open it up to get the chicken out and the fiery air makes you squint and turn away, except in hell there isn't anywhere to turn away because every way you turn God has more fire to punish you. Dad cuts the chicken up into pieces and he prays to thank God for giving us this food, for our use, he says, yes and for us in thy service. Then we can eat, quietly, while dad watches us and tells us what to do.

THE FATHER

So much easier
to choose not to say
what hides anyway
shows itself
only in chapter and verse.

If father loved God
then why didn't love spill over
all those children he made
and mother too
why didn't he need her
all those family years
just climbing up to the pulpit
to say again what the Bible said
and not even that
but a fundamentalist fury
of exegesis

and us stranded in the audience
waiting for him to finish
always waiting for the end
of his sermon or the world
(but hoping for the sermon
because of the once-a-week
chicken dinner slow-baking
in the oven at home)
not to mention hell-fire
which ever remains
the only other choice
for Baptists.

Perhaps a father's love
is suffering
bitter knowledge
unpaid debt.
God doesn't change some things
after all.

Fathers
whose fathers
did not talk to them
probably won't talk
to their own children.
Generations step down like this
poems taking the place of
or roaring through dark winter
wind-of-time howlings
and the silence behind all
that is given
and not freely
though you hear it said.

From way up in the pulpit
Father apologizes
in his general way
says, everybody's human.
And all the families say, Amen.

When the tie goes tight around the child's neck
and shoes are cold stiff leather
and the wool of the suit jacket snags at
the chapped ring of the neck.

When the preacher father glares down
from a high pulpit
and the women are told to sit quietly aside
and the music is about washing in blood and
dark, deep wounds.

When the only seat is a hardwood pew.

When the child needs only to go and pee
but the sermon must first finish with
the promise of perfect bliss or endless torture.

When the old people refuse to smile
at fidgety children during the sermon
and when the preacher talks about
how evil everyone is
even if they seem okay.

When the sermon gets around to speaking
directly to the child and telling how
eternal damnation will spare no one.

When the preacher sneers.

When you decide you can't cry anymore
because somebody might find you out
and discover what you really think.

When Fear adopts you for good.

When you wake in terror
because you have seen Hell and barely survived
and your mother tells you your preacher father
will help you be saved.

When you are saved for the second time.

Then the third.

When you first discover that all children
don't live like this.

When the old people do smile back
and everything goes on as before.

When you realize you want to go outside
and play on The Lord's Day
but you aren't allowed
and you think to yourself:
I'd trade Heaven.

When you have forgotten how to play.

There was a big lake.
You could never see to the other side
waves coming from forever
gnarled driftwood and smooth stones
gulls with their synthesizers
breezes lifting remains and reminders.
Lake of memories, dreamscapes
monster claws near children's toes
surfaces I reach into
looking for my mother and father
her unsettled coasts
flotsam of unsaid and undone
his tempered glass
silent reflections, dank absence.
My steps sink in slippery, small stones
dry-wading the shoreline
the question mark waves
fall on their faces and go under
a father's silence
a dark dome.
Everything is certain, he said
hands calloused, still warm
they hold you on the surface
you are learning to stay above
for your mother.
They will let you go
and hold you and let go again
seagulls screeching
questions filling your mouth with lake.
All you have to do is relax now
give up the earth and tread water
eyes stinging a little
and the universe collapsing.

You can't let go like the neighbour boys did
towed under at the mouth of the river
you cling to the surface
fight the holy dark hauling toward sleep.

You have come back along the beach
because everything is curved back and around.
The language meant to offer you eternal life
slams you up against stone.
Your mouth is full of gravel and seaweed.
Your mother is saying paddle like a dog
as the sun spears the water's side.
You are gushing and sputtering.
You don't remember your father hugged you
you remember he doesn't now.
Mother always floats on her back for hours.
You are in the stones
the stones feel like you
the driftwood bones lie beside you
you are not who you think
you are not who they think
coming back to the beach
you never leave
wading the edge of the question
marking the curve of the day
father and mother alongside
saying, anybody can do it
just let go.

By Duffin's Creek flowing down
ripple-slant Saturday sun
my ten by Marie's twelve years
fingers interlaced, locked on the path
down going ever water
dazzle-diamond, nuclear fission eyes
ear-thump of our feet going down
straw grass swishing legs
airs full with comings and goings
insects and startled frogs
lap of the creek's edge and Marie
leading me down to a place where
willows swirl and sway over waves
wobble of things, trick-slippery stones
and O birdsong all along, twitch and
crackle from just back there
Marie telling me I've never been
where we're going, and I'm listening
following along the serious way
without telling back and Marie pulling
a bit too hard at my tardy ten years
pale pit of gone breath
in my gut and the way her clothes follow
like I do, her hair with me willow trails
and matters

O the helpless blind feel of the mind
by Duffin's Creek
and then she's stopped
with her back to the willow
holding me at arm's length
just breathing is all under the weave
and waves black wash and I know
I won't be able to explain to my friends
why or how or even what went down
Duffin's Creek flowing forever
the way I'll always need
to return to what's left
of beginning again.

THE EVANGELIST

for Jimmy Swaggart

He translates the Bible
for his TV audience
telling everyone
what it means:
like a guitarist
under a tree, he says,
playing one chord
over and over
passersby asking him
why just one chord?
The guitarist smiles
because he knows
and tells them:
all those others
are searching for
the right sound
but I've found it
and he strums again:
Prrrrummm.

So the evangelist smiles
with big, white TV teeth
and says, *the one chord*
is the Holy Bible
and do we understand?
The congregation moans
and cries for him
while he struts
across the stage shaking
his outstretched Bible
like a fist and shouting,
Prrrrummm, Prrrummm.

You see what I'm talking about,
he shouts, his Bible aloft
so there's no confusion:
God's holy Word.
By the television, my phone rings
and it's my mother
but all she'll say is
Prrrummm
and back on the screen
he's grinning right at me
and everyone seems more
than happy.

I click it off
say goodbye to my mother
and sit
silence beside me
frowning.

JESUS SAVES

Now that the Baptists
have given me over to Satan
and the Father Godfather
has condemned me
to eternal fire
I am walking around
free and elated
the sun shining into me
instead of deflecting
through eternity.

The Baptists are either
going to burn me in effigy
or, more likely pray for me
till these last days are
finished
and Jesus returns
to send me to Hell
or hand me another
olive branch to bury
with my blind fingers.

I have walked downwards, sure
and at the foot of the street
by the big forever lake
Jesus jumped me from above
held me down
so all I could see was his face
and the sky all over him
stars heavy
and the blue spark
leaving me blank.

He stared at me
like I was a raped woman
and said
I was not guilty
could keep all
the stars in my eyes.

But what about Baptists,
I asked him
and he looked at me
till we were both full
of silence
and the waves of in between.

I have been sitting quietly because there is a roaring inside me, a Niagara Falls, a raging world wonder, a huge, indoor crashing not altogether unlike the sound of a kitchen faucet turned on full, or a thousand kitchen faucets emptying the sky.

Voices, four or five in a room and others too, further back and coming down in syllables, fragments. Circle of three by the window and circle of two just inside the door; four more on the couch. Circle of one watching an earthquake ripple across the lawn, shaking us from the inside out. Somebody will ask you if you are all right and you will understand. We are all alone together, a family.

We agree that we will appear to be together, or, if need be, forget the fact that we are not together. And we do, in fact, forget the fact, the fact of forgetting. We are together then, like all families, and happy too. We were never altogether not together: just in part, so to speak. For instance, we altogether agree not to say the word 'doubt' in the family, not even allow ourselves to think it because we have agreed without agreeing that it is best and we are decent and believe the Holy Bible, word for word.

My mother has agreed to be convinced because she believes her father was probably convinced and her mother and their parents as well and so it only makes sense that she should attempt to believe what is obviously, simply the truth, torrents sweeping over the edge of consciousness. This is why, when I turn to my mother and say doubt, she must say to me: 'We love you, dear, and you have the devil inside you.'

Father is distant and hovering in the mist from mother's consciousness crashing down like Niagara Falls. What appears to me to be an earthquake, father doesn't seem to notice. He is talking about faith and how he believes he was his father's favourite because when they got angry at one another they agreed not to talk. Well, not exactly agreed but simply stopped talking and in this, agreed to forget the disagreement and to be the type of people who never disagreed and so were happy and favourite.

The noise of something, water tap, Niagara Falls: deafening. You cannot hear the too-loud. More shouting will only produce more silence. All the families line up to see everything going over the edge.

The Undoing

Because it gets to that place
at the edge of a day
the nothing overtakes
with the too much of everything
and no word then
till the one
that unbidden, wells up
from the inner eye
the sitting-there Judge
condemning whatever may be
condemned
and the other I
sulking along after
saying
this isn't right.

Walking blind
in the flesh river of malls
searching the smooth sidewalks
for behindness
talking in I's
to the me alone
and cursing whatever
can't fit into my pocket
or won't.

Right here now
in this deckle-edge day
I begin to word-say
what is undone in the world
and what is coming undone
and could it be
that all the unfathered
wandering men
are undoing like this
since dad got away
to forever-work
and made rules
where poems might have been
and said no
over and over again
till all sons met in malls
and the flowing of clothes
and colours and mall music
rivered them
with the sense-over of you
father
and the not quite hereness
we are, without you still.

LYNX LAKE

Wonder tags along
with happenchance
and won't waylay itself
with all your waiting
at the shore
or your three to four hour
drive north
just to be there in case.
The rolling dice weather too
could end it all before the start
but you wait by the edge
of lapping darkness
and there isn't much
to hold you, is there:
perhaps the forest sounds
or the view into it
(what the child calls
green clouds)
can keep you
or the swaying pickerel weed
or the dip of oars somewhere
and the breeze shapes
in leaves and
over the skin of the lake.

Only then perhaps
if you are there
and hitch your eyes up
the sun might do itself
in shimmers and waves
or the surface of the water
heave up slightly and shift
so your knees ache
for the pine-bed forest floor
and you can't explain
what the green light clouds
do inside
trying to stand alone there
as you are
on two legs
sharp, motionless
and suddenly visible
like the blue heron
standing fifty paces away
on one.

I met her working in the emergency department of a provincial mental hospital, a social worker reading Tolstoy, admitting she hadn't quite finished War and Peace but liked Anna Karenina quite a bit. My Gawd, thought me, and to top it off she liked camping in Algonquin. So I thought, what the heck, why not, and told her I wrote poetry. She nodded at me and said, 'I know, well, it's like, you know, it's like you read it and you don't understand it, like a joke you don't get, or like opera,' she said, 'and I don't have the patience.' 'But there are so many kinds of poetry and how many have you tried?' I pleaded. She smiled: 'How many? Well, just yours really,' she said like she'd been saving it up forever and ever, for just this perfect moment. 'Really, just yours.'

NIGHT BENCH

There is a bench
on the church lawn
by Queen Street
where thinking of you
I watch the steeple clock
change clothes
from noon blues to black.
Cars hollow-follow
into the inky avenue
and endings gather
in streetlamp shadows
under creaky old oaks.

Where are you now?

The midnight shimmer road
washed into absence,
heart's echo
and the swish-whoosh
of cars coming and going.
What if this dark street
would pass just now
like a car or a day going down
letting go
a conch shell
rolling silence in waves,
the shhh-fade
like a back turned
on an early evening
a simple no
and this bench stretched out
with its new place for nobody
and for the nothing
we know better
than each other.

1   The first part had to do with
perfect anatomy
bent over bum
pumping by the streetcar
spandex and lacy shadows.

I should have been following
stanza three in my poetry book
but the eyes peeked out
and o bum
I count the ways.
Then the fat forty tonne streetcar
fell behind so to speak
and her bum into the sunset
city life
disappeared.

2   She was probably eighty
(not the bicycle-bum)
but the woman sitting in front
hair gray and bobby-pinned
instead of brushed
and the mothball essence
at the centre of that dusty
take-along old closet smell
brought my eyes up again
from my book.

Why these diversions,
I was asking myself
when the streetcar blinked
REQUEST STOP and
so I did or tried at least
but it welled up in me
till sorrow sat in too
or a kind of melancholy
abstracting and pulling
out of focus
all the world of my eyes
gauze now
and the rumbling
twenty tonnes of going somewhere
but not knowing anymore
the wheres or whys.

Hands reddened, scratched
by grasping and letting go
grasping again.
Nobody remembers
how long we've been
climbing this tree
but the ground is gone
clouds underfoot and
foliage so thick above
there is no clear
beginning or end left
a middle of things feeling
and the ache of legs'
tedious push and pull
like memory
a children's circle game.
There was a woman
in this tree
but by mistake
I talked too much
said jump
and with regret for both of us
she did:

sun spears in leaves bring
back views
and old songs on breezes
hands so tired of up and down
eyes half-cocked and
wishy-wet with dreams.
What is the reason
for climbing:
why not sit like a guru
under a tree
learn to stop struggling
and accept
the everywhichway
life will be.

SEPARATION

And so
while trees
find their way
in wind
and sun falls
to pieces in leaves
I wait
for something
for any thing or bit
of you
to wander home.

This room is never finished.
Every day I sit here
with words all around me

                                photos of loved ones
                                leaning here and there

empty envelopes

                                      and pictures

Monet's Italian harbour
Vincent's whirling sky
a Group of Seven calendar.

Up in the top corner wall
a bright yarn-spun Bolivian bird
in flight

                                no place permanent

as in the everyday
the vagabond wind
takes along almost anything
it brushes by

                              just set down over there

and then
what you wanted
originally
a room with walls
a door, a big window above

                              and how bit by bit

things were set in place
the window framed and painted
a plant sitting on books
and finally the hum of the Mac
and words blinking

                                  scattered light

across the screen.

With time every little fault
will be uncovered, every dimple
in the drywall, every uneven joint.
The family still leans on the floor
by the wall.
I don't know how to arrange them
can't say what it is I have to tell
only know

                              they must wait here

with me
for the finishing touches
for a last arrangement
where everything is

                              undone

to perfection.

THERAPY

Translucent morning
side-slant sun
sparrows full-chirp in the oak
and traffic other-sounds
swishing into the throat
of the city.

The whole thing waits
in soft-sell whispers
shouting news-hawkers
streetcars every seven minutes
one tax-return per person
a flu a year
every big little thing
leans here
with the weight
of what's unseen, undone.

Clock-talk-purr-walk
the steady zees
of the mind's soft hissing:
I do not know what the sparrows say
with their sudden silence
but wait
for the promise
in standing and listening
the not knowingness
that calls me by name.

Across from me
an old woman nods into stories
I tell her
writes line after line
of lies and not lies in
a generic two-chair rumba
thin venetian blinds
doing a slow hoola to
the rumble of heat ducts.
Beside the woman
an umbrella tree
slowly succumbs
to the clinical view
head bent over
arms slack.
You just know by looking
it can't dance here.

As a line is drawn
which has no beginning
and goes beyond the place
where the eyes have fingers
the waves roll in
one by one to a shore
the everything turning over
and whispering, shhhhhhh,
till another begins
where one never ended.

It might be an ocean's edge
or the way a memory surfaces
and says the same thing
over and over till it isn't
words and images any longer
but the something
which precedes being
and knows anything is possible
anything at all.

As a line drawn along
the earth and the sky
a highway perhaps, or borders
of dawns and dusks rolling
into and out
with sound effects or without
and a lone figure
searching for shells
of things from the everyday,
nameless, forgotten
until the eye claims
what has always been
never this.

I cannot tell you
in simple colours
and familiar schemes
but must hint at
the thing that escapes
being said and done
that senses the posse
of words and dissolves
before they arrive.
Drifting along the beach
you can't avoid
falling into the circularity
of waves rolling, telling you
what's happened to the years
and to the one that comes back
to the mind invited or
not invited
her voice, barely shhhhhhh,
her eyes full of that time
nobody leaves behind
for good.

I go back and forth in it
my legs rubbery, vertigo
of knowing nothing
ever ends
but is only torn in fragments
from the heart
by crushing surf and round wind
hard as apples falling.

Listen, it doesn't matter
which way you go at the edge
of oceans, it doesn't change
what has gone by
and what's in tow for you.
Go ahead, she said,
and dared you to leave
as if you could
and so you did.

It never straightens out
like highways out
of bad towns should
it just keeps turning
the circle of itself
waiting for me
one more time
as if I could turn
around and be the man
you dreamed
looked something like me
and found you resting
at a roadside
or near the waves
coming in
and didn't say the end.

Because he has never found her again
and because longing is religious
with its promise of second-comings
he drives the night freeway
swallowed in full throttle roar silence
dark over memory highways or sideways
hot wind or slashing rain
syncromesh Time shifting
smoothly into the Sixties
those certain streets, houses
where he stops almost
the memories holding course
through all the years
Time has lived there
lawn saplings now closing above.

Because she has not come back
the night sits like this
with slurred senses doing the rounds
like offering plates
clattering with coins
and the weeping that the faithful
offer up with longing hymns
because he has not come to find her
before tonight (nor even now)
as longing holds him gently back
says tomorrow, tomorrow.
The highway night a.m. oldies
gypsy with him, freedom hymns
taking to the road
because he has not found her yet
as roaring joins with roaring
on the freeway home
that is not home again.

I try to remember
sleeping together
how she would reach
from a dream
and without waking
rest her hand on me.
Did it never happen?
I can't forget
an image of her
childhood, sad,
turned to the wall
hugging herself
because there was nobody
who could stop her father
when he would scare
her mother away
and come
for his daughter.

So nowadays
she sleeps curled
into cocoons
safe as can be
which is not safe
though her father
is long dead now
and lovers like me
pull away
feeling too alone
with her
lying beside them.

On my own again
the nothing beside me
holds itself
an absence.
Some nights in bed
I hold her absence to me
and enter it forever.

Dangling Affirmations

Articulated yellow streetcars caterpillar
up Damrak to Hotel Tabu
where the stairs are so steep
you carry your bags above your head
as if on a ladder.

After the all night jet cramp seats
the inside-out plastic food
and the sideshow
in front of Central Station
(hawkers at you with havens and hookers
ornery hungries camped out at the edge
of their teens, quick palm artists, pushers,
shakedown cynics scrounging
with open palms)
you wear your luggage tightly
at the money-changer's window
fingers skedaddling through percentage points
hands glowing
with sunflowers and change.

Across the way two hundred bicycles
are chained to a fence by a canal.
You don't think why just then
but you are giggling with delight
like the hippie tequila kids you just passed
on Leidseplein.
You don't really know where you're going
anymore than they do
climbing the day
and drunk with travelling.

I set down the phrase
'I do not enjoy'
because it fits
this piece of scratch
to be put aside
in faith
in the knowledge
that the fullness of time
will snatch it up again
and again.

Blessed assurance
Jesus is mine
O what a foretaste
but not all the time.

So I set down the phrase
and put it aside
and then
funny thing, Lord
if you don't know already
the April all-atwitter birds
get through to me
just then by my window
little Mozarts in the oak

lah-dee-dah

and it will do
for a drizzly Monday morning
this hope getting particular
and calling me
'cheap'
from the grandstand trees.

Never the thing itself
knocking politely
pamphlets in hand,
but a tree-weave, say,
or a moment of I AM light
haloing the gutter drunk, his hands
almost believing in the bottle.

Whole wind hard as
knowing: this is the voice crying
and this is the wilderness
with pavement.
Sun-knife in cloud-clay,
the blind puppy-search for teat,
warmth of you spooned into me –
it's everywhere and never
the kind of free we buy
but a sort of bluesman plucking
and bending his guitar,
saying Lord-have-mercy
while our shadows fall
to their knees.

O confusion constructs
its highrise dwellings in the heart.
It's all the same, we say,
Don't make no nevermind.

But what of the poem,
what of the music-bus
or the cloak of colours?
What of the reminder
breathing in leaves
or the scripture
of free senses?

Listen to the guitar
praying for us
singing the hymn of itself
in glory.

By saying yes
the wind weaves
canvas in the air
for green sketches.

By saying yes
a spinneret glint stretches
from pepper to tomato
wafting
through lazy geraniums
dancing around with the light
in spindly marigolds.

Yes.
The butterfly
in its schemes of breeze:
the erratic
close-up
is smooth cumulus
inside.
What jangles minds
sculptures
a perfect calm of heart.
Bees gather on sheltered
bloom-blasted fuschia.
They drink and stagger
in the air
ram me aside
and again.

But yes to butter bees
and pepper flies
and clouds up billowing.
Yes to the one brick of
the moment
piled upon another
and the church going up
mortar chewed and trowelled
the shovels and vowels
going up.

There can be a wall
brick by brick
in the heart of a poem
or the side of a hill.
There's likely a web dangling
from the eave of a church
and an oak leaf
dangling in the air's fingers
because of yes.
When growing is these
potted peppers
looking away from the sun
green shoulders swell
out of image and idea.
Hearts are tomatoes
growing on your flat roof
their flowers blooming
all over your sounds and sights.
Yes to the rain of memory
the clatter above
coming down
through the eyes.

Yes to the melting sun
in the shingles
and the wiggling air.
Yes to the preacher
unlocking his door
and to the holy hound
at his heel
the shocked cat
in the tree.

Wind on flesh, the weight
yes and the gap between
having and knowing it
sometime later.

Yes to the spider and snake
and a flat roof
with tar and gravel
and heaps of having
piled against the inevitable.
Yes to the one wall that begins
a temple on a hill.
Yes to the rainbow home of flesh
the hardiness and the melting
the ice and the fire
of today and
oh yes
the words
yes.

Emily Carr prowls
these old oaks
leaving huge swaths

forest green

ochre concoctions
to work strange wonders
with common ailments of the eye

look how the light gushes down
in night rivers

whole canvases sway
like wind-clan trees
in autumn song

crystal solitude

the sound of brush
scratching air

little white church
riding green waves

bold stroke conifers

ancient totems

tiny whitecap skiff
listing toward glory.

SEASONAL RATES OF INTEREST

Think of the cash
of October light
sky hung in amber
all gimme and gold.

Or fire, is it?
Burn-down day
one marigold seeds
a thousand
bloom blaze
burning cities
to the ground.

Fall light overflows
attaches itself
colour of October trees
wind inside out
in cold bones.

Crisp leaves
crunchy grass underfoot
heartbeats and tick-tocks
the clicking of buttons
on sweaters.

Such light inside
the body of things
all giving and glow
leaves lifted
drawn up
by the sky's breathing
pieces of gold.

Near Manikarnika Ghat
a Brahman priest
is sitting forever,
bamboo umbrella
white web overhead.
He is selling flowers
to be offered
at the sacred Ganges:
for a little money
he will coax prayers
out of you, teach
the way down
the many hundred steps.
Sitting cross-legged,
back straight,
his impeccable absence
in dark eyes,
he stares straight ahead
and slightly above me.
Behind him,
dawn or dusk
over the river,
renounced
pink cumulus.

A festival day
steady stream of people,
tributary of colours
rippling down stairs
to the Ganges,
black-haired women
wrapped in neon-pink shawls
or blazing orange,
widows in white,
laughing men in pastel turbans.

At the side of the steps
a white plaster wall
rising two stories
odd, tiny balconies and
jaundice here and there.
The other side is lined
with hawkers
flogging food and
plastic flowers,
everything and nothing.
On a landing halfway down
a skinny cow presides
dumbfounded and holy
in a shawl of flies.
At the foot of a ghat
the festival day
leaves no place untaken
bathers everywhere
queued up the steps as
far as the eye strains.
Only so many can crowd
into the shallows to pray,
wash out clothes and bathe:
hands are cupped ritually and
a sip is taken
the holy, polluted river swallowed
by young and old alike,
poor and poorer.
Here and there, having completed
their cleansing
people sink back to the steps.
Where one retreats
two edge forward.
This is a celebration.
Children howl everywhere.

To die in Benares, it is said,
is to be joined with the eternal,
to end the endless cycle
of death and rebirth,
the crowded heart emptied
into the vast spaces of God.

A beggar squats on Market Street,
a leper wrapped in
dung-coloured blankets and
huddled in the middle of the way.
The cloth is held to the face
and only the eyes appear,
a Hindu woman
hiding both her sex
and her disease.
A swollen hand
in tattered bandages
held out patiently
for stray string-beans
or a handful of rice
for the battered aluminium pot
at her feet.
Close to the dirt
broken charity sits
waiting for God.
Behind her, not ten metres
a young fellow displays
balloons of all colours,
rainbows for sale.

Not far from the market,
a woman in a bright sari
holding a baby in her lap
while she whirls a skein-winder
throwing off wool
for the carpet-makers.
Next door, the carpet-maker
is a ten year old boy,
shiny carbon-black eyes
a hundred miles from home.
On the loom, intricate tapestry,
silks, pink and gold.
On the boy's back
a tattered t-shirt,
his arms far too skinny
to belong to such huge hands.
He does not smile
when I request a photo,
only leans forward
and rests his elbows down
on his work,
and looks up at me
so I cannot miss his ashen lips
in the click of the frame,
my awe and shame.

At the top of the steps
over Manikarnika Ghat
the smoke swirls in veils,
the sweetish smells of
flesh fires, pyres for the dead,
for whatever remains
you bring
to this delirium of the senses.

An old woman descends alone,
barely accomplishing each step.
The Ganges waits
for the living and the dead,
the petalled offerings
of flowers, the ash petals.
The keepers of the crematory,
the Doms dressed in black rags,
are cynical and steal from mourners.
The fires hiss like water spilled
on flame, ash-gray powder
blanketing the ghat
and spread by mourners
over the surface of the river,
beside the swimming celebrants
of Lord Siva,
Death and Life side by side,
skin to skin.
The old woman descends,
does not look up
step after step.
Finally, when she has reached
the bottom
her eyes flicker
as she hobbles into the Ganges.
Nearby, she has seen the Destroyer
but she lives yet and
joins with the living,
the cleansing celebration
at Benares.

She knows
one day will carry her
into fire
and she will be given
to the Ganges
but not today.
Today, she thanks Lord Siva
for the flicker in her eyes,
for the ride down
the hundred steps,
for life hard as it is,
for the grace
bestowed old women with faith
in this holiest city,
this beacon shining,
this manifestation
called flesh.

EPIPHANY

for Michael Bedford-Jones

Do you know what to say
on winter white sunny days
waking from dark sleep
into window light?
Are there words left
to mean this kind of light
in trees
or the wobble
that trees know
in the midst
of things-as-they-are?

The icicled Christmas tree
lies on the lawn
like a king in white robes.

The children
belonging to light
dance for the king
kicking the stars
in the snow
in the sky
in the sun-white winter
height of day
gleaming crystal
with words all around them
and easy grace
without words.

When morning rocks itself
in treetops
and at the edge of knowing
little tellers take their stations
I cock my head up and to the right
to have the light full on my face
and the mere sight of things
that reaches like wings
through wind
spends on me like crazy
I tell you
like some heavenly bank
that just won't stop lending.

And when I gasp and
say, enough
the whole world laughs and heaps
its whelming over at my door
and plainly will not comprehend
any paltry whimpered wanting.

So, okay, says me
Feast it is
and silence gushes in
holding high its golden platter of
onomatopoeia.

THIN-SLICED, FAT OCTOBER TOMATO ON TOASTED WHOLE-WHEAT WITH MAYO AND PEPPER

Pitifully disorganised, overwhelmed by monstrous details and their layered dust, I forgot, this Spring, to plant my roof-top garden until the end of June when Linda, my friend from Mississauga, broke her toaster and in the fixing I became the recipient of three tomato plants. Then, those twice daily, tepid fortified waterings and the yanking of tricky, greedy weeds, the guarding against bulbous glutton hornworms and the nocturnal interloper raccoons. And then there's Glory and Mystery, who come along like the surprise in memory packages, the down deep promise where time blooms into time and old October glows with Vincent's ochres and my very own most red tomatoes.

You cannot purchase the ingredients of the perfect toasted-tomato-on-whole-wheat. It's something that happens over months, perhaps a lifetime, Glory and Mystery, the particular sweetness of sliced October, sliced October light and the building up of the thing at hand: focussed hunger near noon and the run to the garden for a quick-pick and rush to the kitchen, fragrant with butter and browning bread, the arrangement of slices overlapping clockwise, the mayo and black pepper and then, in a stupid hurry, not thinking, a first huge bite even before sitting and Glory and Mystery, the sweetness of it thrills straight through and stops me in the middle of the kitchen floor to wow and flutter, wait for an instant replay, take another bite and another, images of beloved toasters in bite three, midnight garden standoffs with whole families of raccoons in bite five, and that no specific sweetness that should have a new name for every time it comes to discover us again.

Everything is impossibly complicated and yet the light of the whole world bending into the new day smiles at me like a simple child and hangs around like I'm the only thing it has to do today. And another guy I know is up the hill from me loading words together just as I am and the sun is there too and he's probably noticing how it warms up to him. All over the new day folks are absorbing this chance in myriad ways, a glance and pause by the bathroom window, a neck bared as if to a lover's kiss, an inner wrist turned up like warm, spilt milk. Those you might think you could ask about this will not be able to tell you what you need to know. Even the gentle gurus give away mirrors to their most beloved. Fear not, said the angel of light, for I bring you great tidings and joy that will be abused and forever twisted by the gaggled churches and honking priests. The fundamental truth is all they emphatically ignore, all they pull you away from when they put their arms around you and teach you the words to their songs. See how the sun comes down like it needs you to be there, a resting place. You are related to light. Let someone else say God and hit you on the side of the head with their scriptures. I just want to tell you about the appearance of sunbeams in this neighbourhood, maybe laugh a little bit about it or wait together, to see.

ACKNOWLEDGEMENTS

'Benares' was published in *Event*, Volume 2, number 22.
'Traveller' and 'After the Ground Goes' were published in *Matrix*,
number 40. 'Dangling Affirmations From a Flat Church Roof'
was published in *Poetry Canada*, Volume 12, number 2. 'Sunday
Dinner' was published in *Prairie Fire*, Volume 15, number 1.

The author wishes to acknowledge the support of The Ontario
Arts Council.

Special thanks to Barry Dempster, Karen Ruttan and Donna
Jansen.

Thanks also to Avrom Isaacs, who procured the transparency of
William Kurelek's painting. This work was taken from *Kurelek's
Vision of Canada*, Hurtig Publishers, Edmonton, 1983. The book
carried Kurelek's commentary alongside most pictures. For this
painting, a self-portrait, he simply quoted a verse from the Book
of John 3: 8, 'The wind breathes where it will, and thou canst
hear the sound of it, but knowest nothing of the way it came or
the way it goes; so it is, when a man is born by the breath of the
Spirit.'

BRIAN VANDERLIP was born in 1952 in Cobourg, a small Ontario town in which his father was a Baptist minister. Educated in child development, his work experience includes various group homes and the Ministry of Health. He now lives in Holland Landing, Ontario with his wife, and is employed in the emergency department of a Toronto psychiatric hospital.

His poetry has been widely published in Canada over the past two decades, including *More Garden Varieties*, a League of Canadian Poets' anthology of prize-winning poems. He is also a frequent reviewer for *Poetry Canada Review*.

His first book of poetry, *What Happens to Memory*, was published in 1989.